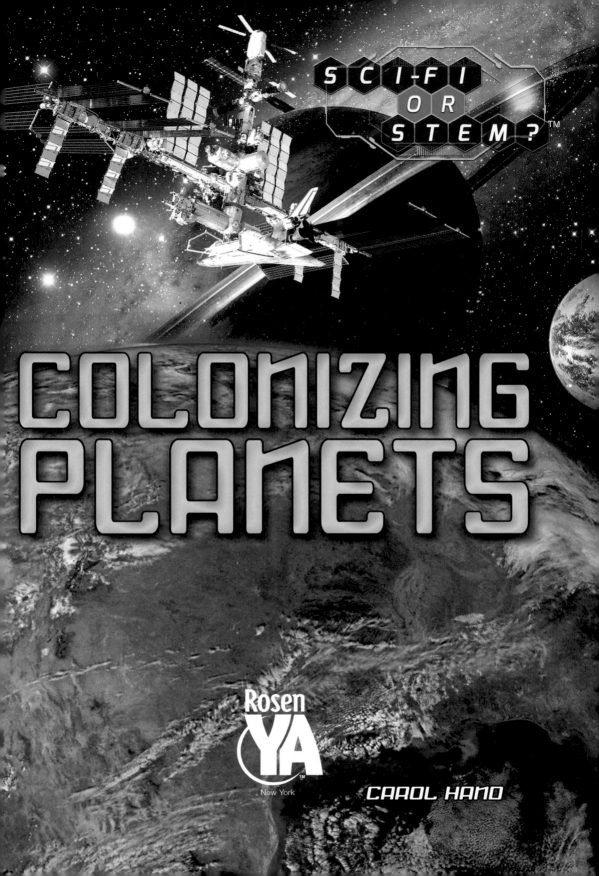

SCI-FI OR STEM?™

COLONIZING PLANETS

Rosen
YA
New York

CAROL HAND

Published in 2019 by The Rosen Publishing Group, Inc.
29 East 21st Street, New York, NY 10010

First Edition

Library of Congress Cataloging-in-Publication Data

Names: Hand, Carol, 1945– author.
Title: Colonizing planets / Carol Hand.
Description: New York : Rosen Publishing, 2019. | Series: Sci-Fi or STEM? | Audience: Grades 7–12. | Includes bibliographical references and index.
Identifiers: LCCN 2017044425| ISBN 9781508180296 (library bound) | ISBN 9781508180302 (pbk.)
Subjects: LCSH: Space colonies—Juvenile literature. | Habitable planets—Juvenile literature. | Space environment—Juvenile literature. | Outer space—Exploration—Juvenile literature.
Classification: LCC TL795.7 .H36 2019 | DDC 629.44/2—dc23
LC record available at https://lccn.loc.gov/2017044425

Manufactured in the United States of America

CONTENTS

As his crew attempts to evacuate the planet to avoid a coming storm, Astronaut Mark Watney is blown away from the others and injured. Thinking he is dead, the other astronauts leave him behind. Stranded alone on Mars, Watney must use his wits to signal his crew and the National Aeronautics and Space Administration (NASA) that he is alive—and more important, figure out how to stay alive until he is rescued. This sequence of events is the plot of the 2015 movie *The Martian*, based on a book of the same name by Andy Weir. In an article in *The Guardian*, Dr. Robert Zubrin, founder of the Mars Society, wrote that *The Martian* is the first movie that attempts a realistic depiction of life on Mars and the problems astronauts are likely to encounter. Just how realistic is it, though?

The biggest error is the dust storm at the movie's beginning. Martian atmospheric pressure is much too low to generate such a violent storm. According to NASA scientist Dave Lavery, although Mars has dust storms of one hundred miles per hour (160 kmh) or more, they are similar to winds of only eleven miles per hour (18 kmh) on Earth. Author Weir readily admitted this inaccuracy. He used it as a plot device to strand Watney on the planet.

This view of Wdowiak Ridge was taken by the Mars *Opportunity* rover. The stranded Watney would have seen such views. The rover's tire tracks are visible at right.

Another scientific inaccuracy involves gravity. The low gravity on Mars would cause astronauts to hop, as they did on the moon, rather than walk normally. Also, the movie does not discuss methods for protecting Watney from radiation. Given radiation levels on Mars, he might have become very ill or died of cancer shortly after returning to Earth. Some inaccuracies are relatively minor. For example, there would be no space-walking astronaut waving his arms to guide the docking of a remote-controlled supply vehicle.

What did the movie get right? The inflatable Martian habitat, or Hab, in which Watney spends much of the movie, is relatively accurate. A similar habitat, the Bigelow Aerospace module, was tested on the International Space Station (ISS) in 2016. Watney, a botanist, set up a greenhouse to grow potatoes from stocks brought by the crew. He used Martian soil fertilized with stored human waste. This combination would work quite well, as would Watney's chemical method for producing water to grow the potatoes. However, Zubrin pointed out that Watney might have baked water from ice in the Martian soil. (His personal water needs were met by recycling urine and other water in the Hab—similar to the water recovery system used in the ISS.) Watney's rover is similar to NASA's Multi-Mission Space Exploration Vehicle (MMSEV). He restored communication with Earth by scavenging parts from an actual Martian probe that stopped transmitting in 1997. That solution is also quite possible, said Lavery.

Overall, *The Martian* gives a fairly realistic glimpse of life on Mars. Such flights of imagination have fueled the work of real scientists for generations. As renowned theoretical physicist Stephen Hawking wrote in the introduction to Lawrence M. Krauss's book *The Physics of Star Trek*, "There is a two-way trade between science fiction and science. Science fiction suggests ideas that scientists incorporate into their theories, but sometimes science turns up notions that are stranger than any science fiction." Young people aspiring to enter space science still devour science fiction (sci-fi). But to learn real science, they must also delve into science, technology, engineering, and mathematics (STEM) courses. Any future space colonist will need thorough preparation in these academic fields.

CHAPTER 1

IMAGINING COLONIZATION

In hard science fiction, science and technology shape the story world. The science may be an extension of modern science or based on hypothetical science that might someday exist. In soft science fiction, science may be essential to the story, but the details (of say, faster-than-light travel) are assumed rather than explained. The story concentrates on the sociology or politics of the imaginary world. Great sci-fi contains elements of both. As writer Anthony Gramuglia explained in his article on the history of science fiction, "Throughout its span, sci-fi asks where we are as a species, where we will go, and what will happen when we get there." Often, science follows where science fiction leads. For example, what if humans could colonize other planets?

EARLY SCIENCE FICTION

Through the mid-1800s, most science fiction writers set their stories on Earth, which was still relatively unexplored. Perhaps the greatest writer of such adventure stories was Jules Verne.

Verne ventured off the planet in his classic tale *From the Earth to the Moon* (1865). His hard-science calculations of the speed of his moon launch were similar to calculations for the *Apollo 11* moon launch, more than a century later. In H. G. Wells's 1898 sci-fi novel *The War of the Worlds*, Martians with highly sophisticated technology invade Earth. Wells used soft science fiction to criticize British imperialism, the policy of invading, conquering, and colonizing other countries. He asked imperialists, "How would you feel if someone did the same to you?"

In the late 1800s, astronomers discovered channels on Mars, which some interpreted as canals built by an ancient Martian

This illustration shows the moon vehicle imagined by Jules Verne in his 1865 novel, *From the Earth to the Moon*. The vehicle, a gigantic cannon, would not have worked.

civilization. This discovery led to a flurry of science fiction based on imagined Martian civilizations. In 1912, Edgar Rice Burroughs serialized *A Princess of Mars* in a sci-fi monthly magazine, and in 1917, he published it in book form. Its hero, John Carter, was an Earth "invader" who later became the hero of the 2012 Disney movie *John Carter*. Burroughs's work celebrated the white colonialism that Wells criticized. White men (never women) visited other planets, took over, and became leaders of the (always inferior) alien race. In the low gravity of Mars, Carter had extraordinary strength compared to Martians and became a great warlord. Pop culture scholar Jess Nevins says Carter was the basis for today's superheroes. But Burroughs also made Mars seem like a real place that humans could visit. A century later, space programs around the world are planning actual Mars missions.

SCI-FI TAKES OFF

Sci-fi in the first half of the twentieth century was dominated by fun, but nonscientific, "space operas" set on Mars or other planets. Later works, including Ray Bradbury's 1950 book of interconnected stories, *The Martian Chronicles*, were more serious. Bradbury describes human attempts to colonize Mars and the response of the advanced Martian civilization. Isaac Asimov's Foundation series describes a vast galactic empire spanning millennia, with colonized planets throughout the galaxy. Its seven books were published between 1942 and 1993. Asimov created a branch of mathematics called psychohistory that could predict the future, if applied on a galactic scale. Although psychohistory is well documented in the books, the ability to travel through the galaxy is assumed. As economist (and fan) Paul Krugman noted

This still is from the 1984 movie *Dune*, directed by David Lynch. *Dune* was one of many sci-fi books and movies of the time featuring fictional worlds with well-developed ecologies—in *Dune*'s case, a desert.

in his article about how Asimov's Foundation books grounded his economics, "The Foundation novels are about society, not gadgets … they're about societies that don't seem much affected by technological progress."

Frank Herbert's 1965 novel *Dune* was set on the desert planet Arrakis. The novel and its later movie adaptation describe a civilization built to harvest the spice called mélange, which makes long-distance space travel possible (and coincidentally lengthens life spans). The novel and its sequels concentrate on the planet's politics and social systems, but also carefully describe the desert ecology of Arrakis and how its giant sandworms—and people—adapt to it.

Ursula K. Le Guin, a prolific writer of twentieth century science fiction, created the Hainish series of novels, describing humanity's colonization of several nearby planets. Her tales, including *Rocannon's World* (1966), *The Left Hand of Darkness* (1969), and *The Dispossessed* (1974), approach civilizations through their sociology and anthropology. They are also rich with descriptions of the ecology of her alien worlds.

Star Trek introduced space exploration to the general public. Here, the main characters, Kirk, Spock, and McCoy (*left*), are shown in the episode "The City on the Edge of Forever."

STAR TREK AND STAR WARS

Most early sci-fi television series and movies were rather forgettable—until the advent of two entertainment concepts that took colonization of other planets for granted. *Star Trek* and *Star Wars* began in 1966 and 1977, respectively. They made science fiction a part of popular culture. Faster-than-light travel, alien life-forms, and alien planets—both Earthlike and not—are staples of these universes. Regular people, not just science fiction writers and their fans, began to think seriously about traveling to the stars and to assume it would happen someday.

George Lucas changed the face of science fiction with the creation of *Star Wars*. Writer and sci-fi historian Gramuglia said the release of the first *Star Wars* movies led to a resurgence in science fiction that spawned the television series *Battlestar Galactica*, *Star Trek* spin-offs and movies, the *Dune* movie, and the movie *E.T. The Extraterrestrial*. The writers of *Star Wars* took pains to make their planets, colonies, and aliens realistic. On Listverse.com, Andy Roberts listed ten planets

Star Wars Episode II: Attack of the Clones was set on a desert planet much like Mars. Part of the movie was filmed in Africa's Tunisian Desert.

SCI-FI SOURCES: *STAR TREK*

The opening of *Star Trek*'s second series (1987–94), *Star Trek: The Next Generation*, describes the goal of the entire saga: "Space: the final frontier. These are the voyages of the starship *Enterprise*. Its continuing mission: to explore strange new worlds, to seek out new life and new civilizations, to boldly go where no one has gone before." Gene Roddenberry pitched the concept for the original television show as an adventure series—a Western set in outer space. But he really wanted to tackle social issues, such as prejudice, racism, and war in a way that would make viewers think, without threatening or preaching.

The first series, which originally aired from 1966 to 1969, pushed boundaries—for example, *Star Trek* gave viewers television's first interracial kiss. It predicted equality and a loss of prejudice among humans and technology that improved everyone's lives. Captain James T. Kirk explains to a twentieth-century man who has been revived from cryogenic sleep, "A lot has changed in the past three hundred years. People are no longer obsessed with the accumulation of things. We've eliminated hunger, want, the need for possessions. We've grown out of our infancy." The *Star Trek* universe assumes freedom, equality, kindness, and decency. Marvelous technology abounds, from the warp drive that allows instantaneous faster-than-light travel, to transporters that "beam" a person's molecules to a new location and reassemble them. But the original series' beloved character Mr. Spock had no illusions about the limits of technology. In the 1966 episode, "The Naked Time," he comments, "Instruments register only those things they're designed to register. Space still contains infinite unknowns."

in the *Star Wars* universe that actually exist in our own. Alderaan 2.0, the home of Princess Leia, almost exactly matches Earth. Geonosis, site of the first battle in the clone wars (*Episode II: Attack of the Clones*) is a twin of Mars. The gas giant Bespin, home to the huge floating Cloud City, mirrors Kepler-86c, an exoplanet 1,200 light-years from Earth. Other *Star Wars* planets resemble moons of Jupiter and Saturn.

REACHING FOR THE STARS

Modern science fiction uses scientific knowledge of Mars, gained through satellites and landers, to develop more accurate stories of its colonization. Kim Stanley Robinson authored a trilogy of books in the 1990s: *Red Mars*, *Green Mars*, and *Blue Mars*. These books describe the centuries-long process of colonizing and terraforming the lifeless planet, making it habitable for humans. Robinson also describes the social and political changes that occur on Mars and its interactions with Earth.

The Coyote series, by Allen M. Steele, follows Earth's first group of interplanetary colonists. When the first book opens in 2070, Earth is controlled by a repressive government. The captain and crew hijack the spacecraft, replacing intended colonists with political dissidents and their families. They travel in cold sleep for 250 years to reach the interplanetary moon Coyote, more than forty light-years from Earth. Later books describe the problems of colonizing an alien planet, the politics of developing a new society, and interactions with existing life-forms. The series strives for scientific, social, and political plausibility.

Sci-fi writers have turned out thousands of books, movies, and television shows that imagine colonizing other worlds. They will continue to do so. Imagining something is the first step to making it a reality. Stories of colonizing other planets kindle excitement in young readers, some of whom later become scientists, engineers, and astronauts. Many problems faced by colonists in science fiction will be faced by real colonists. They may not solve these problems the way fiction writers do, but great science fiction opens minds to the possibilities.

CHAPTER 2

WORKING UP TO COLONIZATION

much science fiction is written as though the hard work of colonization is already done. But it has barely begun in the real world. In the coming decades, humans may visit and colonize the moon, Mars, and perhaps asteroids. However, visits to planets outside the solar system are in the far future, if they happen at all. Twenty-first century humans lack the technology required to reach planets in deep space.

WHY COLONIZE OTHER PLANETS?

People understand that space travel and colonizing planets will be difficult and dangerous. For some, this is part of the attraction. They seek more freedom or space than is available on Earth. They seek adventure, and what is more adventurous than being a pioneer on a planet no human has set foot on? Striking out for new planets appeals to those who want to leave civilization behind and seek their destiny in the stars.

Colonizing new planets would provide an incredible boost to science. Studying human adaptation to a new planet would advance biology and biochemistry. Scientists would gain knowledge of geology, chemistry, ecology, and atmospheric sciences by comparing processes on new planets with those on Earth. For example, scientists think both Mars and Venus once had Earth-like atmospheres. Knowing why they changed would help people understand how humans affect Earth.

Colonizing new planets would also advance human civilization. Earth is not likely to run out of energy sources—wind, solar, and other alternative technologies will probably replace depleted fossil fuels. But asteroid mining for precious metals would ease Earth's resource limitations. Furthermore, growing populations ensure Earth will run out of land to colonize. On new worlds, humans could experiment with planetary change, or terraforming, without endangering the home planet.

Finally, many people think colonizing other planets could provide assurance against catastrophes on Earth. It could save

TRAPPIST-1 is an ultra-cool dwarf star in the constellation Aquarius. It has seven earth-sized planets (shown in this artist's conception) that orbit close to the star and to one another.

human civilization and other Earth species. According to Robin McKie in *The Guardian*, Stephen Hawking said, "Life on Earth is at the ever-increasing risk of being wiped out by a disaster such as sudden global warming, nuclear war, a genetically engineered virus or other dangers ... I think the human race has no future if it doesn't go into space."

FIRST STEPS INTO SPACE

Humans have already laid much of the groundwork for colonizing other planets. The Soviet Union's launch of *Sputnik I* on October 4, 1957, proved that humans could build rockets capable of sending objects into space and successfully put artificial satellites into orbit. The United States responded to the Soviet Union's space successes by creating NASA on July 29, 1958. For the next several decades, the two powers competed, both making advances in space technology once thought impossible.

The crowning achievement of the US space program was the Apollo moon landing program. On July 20, 1969, *Apollo 11* astronauts Neil Armstrong and Edwin "Buzz" Aldrin became the first humans to walk on the moon. Subsequently, the Apollo program completed five more successful moon landings. They showed that people could successfully reach, land on, and return from another celestial body.

After the excitement of reaching the moon, space programs became more routine and practical. Earth-orbiting satellites began to proliferate. By April 2017, according to the Union of Concerned Scientists, 1,459 spy, weather, and communication satellites orbited Earth. Scientists also study the universe using huge

Apollo 11 astronauts landed on the Moon on July 20, 1969. Shown here are lunar module pilot Edwin Aldrin, the American flag, part of the module, and astronauts' footprints (*foreground*).

orbiting telescopes, such as the Hubble Space Telescope and the Chandra X-Ray Observatory. NASA sends probes to the outer reaches of the solar system. *Pioneer 10*, bound for Jupiter, was launched in 1972. Its first achievement was successfully crossing the asteroid belt between Mars and Jupiter, which many astronomers had considered impassible. It flew past Jupiter, transmitting the first observations of the giant planet and kept traveling, leaving the solar system in 1983. When last heard from in 2003, *Pioneer 10* was 7.6 billion miles (12.2 billion km) from Earth.

EXPLORING THE SOLAR SYSTEM

Before doing human missions, space scientists must gather as much information as possible about potential worlds to colonize. They develop and test the technology needed to explore or live on these new worlds.

The development of rovers, or vehicles that can travel across the surface of the moon or a planet, sped up discovery on the moon and Mars. Astronauts on the last three Apollo missions drove an electric Lunar Roving Vehicle (LRV) over the moon's surface. Mars

Scientific research is an important activity on the ISS. Here, an astronaut does microgravity experiments involving metformin—a diabetes drug that scientists hope can be repurposed to treat cancer.

rovers are robotic. Four different Mars rovers have landed safely and traveled independently. Two of them, *Opportunity* and *Curiosity*, were still operating in 2017. These roving science laboratories have collected massive amounts of information on Martian geology, water, chemistry, and the possibility of the existence of life. This information will be invaluable when people finally visit Mars.

The space shuttle program, which flew vehicles with crews from 1981 through 2011, operated the first reusable spacecraft. The space shuttle's technological breakthroughs included a heat shield that allowed the shuttle to reenter Earth's atmosphere without burning up

RASSOR, THE ROVER

On moon voyages, astronauts carried enough fuel for the return trip. But carrying fuel for Mars trips would be very expensive because it would add so much weight to the spacecraft. It would also be impractical for Mars colonists to replenish other supplies by bringing them from Earth. What if colonists could mine Mars for resources? NASA's newest rover will make this possible. The Regolith Advanced Surface Systems Operations Robot (RASSOR, pronounced "razor") will mine rocket fuel components, water, and oxygen from the planet's surface. Its bucketlike wheels dig into soil, collect it, and deposit it in an oven for processing. Its wheel drums create traction by rotating in opposite directions. RASSOR will be much tougher than *Curiosity*. It will travel five times faster, carry out sixteen-hour shifts for several years, and haul back forty pounds (18 kg) of soil per trip.

and a new type of landing (gliding in to land on a runway, rather than splashing down into the ocean). The shuttle became a supply ship for the ISS. The ISS was built entirely in space and has had a crew of six continually on board since November 2, 2000. The ISS and its predecessors have shown that people can live for extended periods of time in space.

WHAT'S NEXT?

Humans have the basic technology to visit other bodies in the solar system—especially the moon and Mars. Space experts say a NASA Mars mission could occur by 2030. However, colonizing is a trickier process. Temperature extremes, radiation, and unbreathable atmospheres present serious challenges. Colonists would need to live underground or in leak-proof habitats and would require space suits on the surface. Then, there is the issue of long-term water and food supplies. Mars has water, but it may be difficult to obtain. NASA engineers are working on food supply problems. Ultimately, turning Mars into a livable planet would require terraforming, including raising the temperature and changing the atmosphere. This process would require decades or more, and there is no guarantee of success.

But, despite the obstacles, NASA and several private companies are pushing to explore and colonize other planets, especially Mars. These companies include SpaceX, Mars One (a Dutch nonprofit), Blue Origin, and Bigelow Aerospace. The European Space Agency (ESA) and individual countries including Russia, China, and the United Arab Emirates are exploring and planning to colonize space. The human species is expanding outward.

CHAPTER 3

BASIC ISSUES IN COLONIZATION

By June 2017, NASA's Kepler Space Telescope had discovered 4,034 likely exoplanets (planets outside this solar system) and confirmed 2,335 of them. At least forty-nine of them may be Earth sized and habitable. These exoplanets, however, are hundreds or thousands of light-years distant. Humans are unlikely to visit them in the twenty-first, or even twenty-second, century. In the near future, the emphasis will be on colonizing the solar system. Even that will be challenging.

THE GOLDILOCKS ZONE

The Goldilocks zone, or habitable zone, is the region around a star where life can exist. That is, it has a temperature range in which water can remain liquid. This calculation is determined by the planet's distance from its star. The planet's atmosphere is also important. Both Venus and Mars are technically within the solar system's Goldilocks zone. But the very thick carbon dioxide atmosphere on Venus traps the sun's energy, causing a runaway greenhouse effect. This process makes it far too hot

KEPLER AND K2

Planet hunters use the Kepler Space Telescope, launched in March 2009, to detect exoplanets in a small sliver of space. The several thousand exoplanets Kepler detected during its four-year mission included small, Earthlike planets. These appear to be abundant in the galaxy. In May 2013, a malfunction ended the original Kepler project, but by August, scientists had developed a workaround to continue using Kepler. This new project, K2, is expected to continue through 2018. So far, K2 has discovered three dozen new exoplanets, with more than 250 planet candidates not yet confirmed. Kepler's replacement, Transiting Exoplanet Survey Satellite (TESS), launches in May 2018. TESS will monitor a region of sky four hundred times larger than that of Kepler.

for life. Mars's very thin atmosphere traps little or no heat, making it extremely cold. If the atmosphere of either planet could be adjusted, either could support life.

NASA always looks for water when exploring moons and planets. Liquid oceans almost certainly exist on Jupiter's moon Europa and Saturn's moon Enceladus. Oceans may also exist on Ganymede and Callisto (moons of Jupiter), and on the dwarf planet Ceres. Perhaps most important for potential colonization, Mars has polar ice caps, and possibly running water both above and below ground.

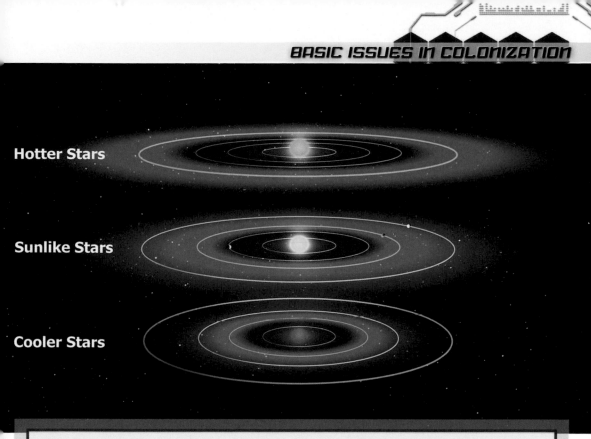

Hotter Stars

Sunlike Stars

Cooler Stars

The Goldilocks zone (shown in green) varies in distance from the star according to the star's temperature. For hot stars, it is much farther away than for cool stars.

THE RADIATION PROBLEM

All space colonists will be exposed to radiation. Highly energetic radioactive particles pass through skin, damaging cells and DNA, the genetic material. People exposed to large doses of radiation in a short time will die from acute radiation poisoning. Individuals receiving small doses over a long time (chronic exposure) risk cancer later in life.

Radiation comes from two sources. The sun releases solar energetic particles (SEPs) during solar flares. Constant but low doses of galactic cosmic rays (GCRs) originate outside the solar system (for example, from exploding stars and pulsars). GCRs are highly

COLONIZING VENUSIAN SKIES

Chris Jones, of NASA's Space Mission Analysis Branch, says that "probably the most Earth-like environment that's out there" exists about thirty-one miles (50 km) above Venus. NASA has a detailed plan for a permanent colony in the sky above Venus, called the High Altitude Venus Operational Concept (HAVOC). Temperatures there range from 32 to 122 degrees Fahrenheit (0 to 50°C). Pressure is similar to Earth's pressure. The Venusian atmosphere would protect colonists from radiation, and oxygen is buoyant (like helium on Earth). Thus, blimplike inflatable habitats could be used as living space. Oxygen and solar energy would be readily available, but water and metal resources would not. A Venusian sky habitat would be livable but not self-sufficient.

energetic and therefore highly damaging. On Earth, organisms are protected from most radiation by Earth's magnetic field and by the atmosphere. The ISS is in low earth orbit, inside Earth's magnetic field, so it is protected from most radiation. But there is no protection outside Earth's atmosphere and magnetic field. Mars has no magnetic field and a very thin atmosphere. The moon has no atmosphere and a very weak magnetic field. Neither is well protected from radiation.

NASA spacecraft are studying the sun's emissions to determine how solar radiation affects the space environment. The Mars *Curiosity* rover carried a Radiation Assessment Detector, or RAD. The RAD made detailed measurements of radiation exposure during the

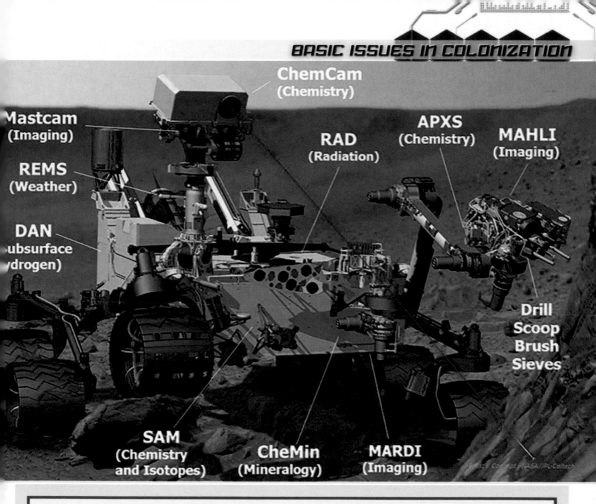

ChemCam
(Chemistry)

Mastcam
(Imaging)

RAD
(Radiation)

APXS
(Chemistry)

MAHLI
(Imaging)

REMS
(Weather)

DAN
subsurface
ydrogen)

**Drill
Scoop
Brush
Sieves**

SAM
(Chemistry
and Isotopes)

CheMin
(Mineralogy)

MARDI
(Imaging)

The car-sized *Curiosity* rover landed on Mars on August 6, 2012. It was fitted for analyzing many aspects of the Martian environment, including radiation levels (measured by the RAD).

trip and on Mars. It showed that, during the 360-day round trip to and from Mars, astronauts would receive more than the lifetime acceptable amount of radiation. Time on the surface would further increase this amount.

SHELTER FROM RADIATION

Spacecraft in the 2010s are fairly well shielded from SEPs, less so from cosmic rays. They contain smaller, heavily shielded areas (radiation "storm shelters"), where astronauts remain during dangerous periods, such as massive solar flares. But keeping space travelers and colonists safe over the long term will require improved science and technology. The best protection would involve highly efficient shielding materials.

NASA is researching several possible materials. As reported by NASA science writer Sarah Frazier, according to Jonathan Pellish, a space radiation engineer at NASA's Goddard Space Flight Center, "The best way to stop particle radiation is by running that energetic particle into something that's a similar size." Hydrogen is one such material. Scientists are considering common

NASA scientists have shown that boron nitride nanotubes (BNNTs) efficiently absorb neutrons produced by space radiation. They are working on a new, less expensive method of producing BNNTs.

materials, such as water and plastics, which contain large amounts of hydrogen. But the ideal material would be used to build the spacecraft, as well as shield it against radiation. NASA is working on structures called hydrogenated boron nitride nanotubes, or hydrogenated BNNTs. These tiny tubes are extremely strong, even at high heat, so they are ideal for both purposes. BNNTs are even flexible enough to make into yarn. Thus, they might also be used in manufacturing space suits and habitats. Further in the future, engineers might even learn to use force fields to produce a protective bubble around a spacecraft, similar to Earth's magnetic field (or the deflector shields on *Star Trek*'s starship *Enterprise*).

THE GRAVITY OF THE SITUATION

People take gravity for granted. A rock rolls downhill. Objects fall down, not up. Feet stay on the ground. But astronauts outside of Earth's atmosphere quickly become aware of gravity—or its absence. Floating in zero gravity (zero-G) in an orbiting spacecraft is fun, but humans are adapted to Earth's gravity. The zero-G of space causes significant changes in body strength and functions. The low gravities of smaller bodies such as the moon and Mars would likely cause similar changes.

In low or zero gravity, muscles waste away quickly. Up to 20 percent of total muscle mass can disappear. As much as 40 to 60 percent of total bone mass can be lost. On Earth, blood follows gravity; thus, blood pressure is much higher in the feet than in the head. In space, without gravity, this gradient vanishes. Astronauts' faces puff up and their legs become thinner. Blood pressure in the

The Advanced Resistive Exercise Device (ARED) helps astronauts keep in shape. Here, European Space Agency astronaut Samantha Cristoforetti exercises on the ISS.

head increases, signaling the body that it has too much blood. After a few days of weightlessness, the body loses up to 22 percent of its blood volume. The heart pumps less and becomes weaker. Back on Earth, the astronaut eventually recovers (except possibly for bone loss), but recovery is challenging.

Astronauts try to maintain body strength in space by doing resistance exercises. On Earth, resistance exercises strengthen skeletal muscles by causing them to contract, using either body weight alone or added weights. In zero-G, to maintain strength, the amount of resistance must equal the astronaut's Earth weight. To add strength or build muscle, additional weights must be used. The Advanced Resistive Exercise Device (ARED) is a series of piston-driven vacuum cylinders and a flywheel that can provide up to six hundred pounds (272 kg) of resistance for bar and 250 pounds (113 kg) for cable exercise. It connects to a computer on the ISS and helps crew members monitor their own exercise programs. The LBNP (Lower Body Negative Pressure) device consists of a chamber containing a treadmill. The suction of a vacuum cleaner lowers pressure in the chamber. The LBNP allows astronauts to exercise at weights of 100 to 120 percent of their weight on Earth. This capability helps maintain muscle and bone function. It also helps cardiovascular function by increasing blood pressure in the legs, which restores the blood pressure gradient.

The moon, Mars, and other space bodies, including orbiting space stations, will each present colonists with a unique set of problems. But all space colonists will require food, water, and livable temperatures, and all must deal with radiation and gravity.

CHAPTER 4

STARTING NEARBY: THE MOST LIKELY NEW HOMES

Nearby bodies are easiest to colonize, so space scientists are concentrating on plans to colonize the moon and Mars. Some people, such as Dr. Robert Zubrin, think explorers should bypass the moon and proceed straight to Mars. Others point out that, because the moon is much closer, colonizing it would be cheaper and easier and should be done first. Either approach requires considerable planning and technology.

COLONIZING THE MOON

Sam Dinkin, writing for *The Space Review*, favors colonizing the moon. Because it is much closer than Mars, less fuel would be needed to reach it. Hundreds of supply missions to the moon are possible in the time needed to make one round trip to Mars. In an emergency, rescue would be much easier than rescue from Mars. Knowledge gained from moon colonization could be used in planning colonization of Mars and more distant planets. Finally, moon colonies could pay for themselves through economic ventures, such as tourism and video entertainment (for example, moon sports).

This photo of moonrise, with the curve of Earth below, was taken from the ISS. Its closeness to Earth makes the Moon an ideal first step for space colonization.

A 2015 study conducted by two space nonprofit organizations, and reviewed by NASA, found that the cost of returning to the moon is 90 percent less than previously estimated ($10 billion rather than $100 billion). Partners on a moon venture would include NASA, international groups such as the ESA, and private companies. Already existing nonspace technology would decrease the cost, according to NASA astrobiologist Chris McKay, as reported by ScienceAlert journalist Fiona MacDonald. Settlers would reach the moon on SpaceX's *Big Falcon* rocket (BFR) and live and work in inflatable habitats made by Bigelow Aerospace. Human waste processed by recycling toilets would fertilize the soil in food-producing habitats. Three-dimensional (3D) printers would produce other supplies. A lunar mining town would use robots to mine hydrogen and water from the lunar crust. The project also employs reusable spacecraft and lunar landers. Ten settlers could be in place by 2022, with one hundred permanent residents a decade later.

Two private companies, Moon Express (MoonEx) and Rocket Lab, are hoping for a soft landing on the moon sometime in 2018. The *MX-1E* lander would be launched on Electron, a launch vehicle built by Rocket Lab. The Electron takes the lander into low earth orbit. The lander then fires its own launchers to land on the moon. This lander would be the first single-stage spacecraft to reach the moon from low earth orbit. It's a tall order; the Electron's first launch occurred in May 2017. But MoonEx cofounder Bob Richards told Jay Bennett of *Popular Mechanics* in 2017, "Everybody thinks something is impossible until they see it done."

COLONIZING MARS

As noted by Leah Ginsberg of CNBC, SpaceX founder Elon Musk believes that colonizing Mars is essential for human survival. "There will be some eventual extinction event," said Musk. He added that survival requires that humans become a multiplanetary species, and Mars is the logical choice for the second planet. In September 2017, as reported in the *New York Times*, Musk announced a new rocket and spaceship to replace all earlier versions. The BFR, will be smaller (only three-fourths the size of an earlier design, called the *Falcon Heavy* rocket). For Mars colonization, it will boost a spaceship carrying about one hundred people into orbit and then return to its launching pad. The spaceship will pick up fuel in orbit and continue to Mars. The BFR can also work near Earth—orbiting multiple satellites at once, carrying astronauts and cargo to the ISS, landing on the moon, and even making long-distance trips between

Elon Musk presents his Mars colonization plan at the International Astronautical Congress in Adelaide, Australia, in September 2017. Above him is a model of SpaceX's proposed gigantic rocket, the BFR.

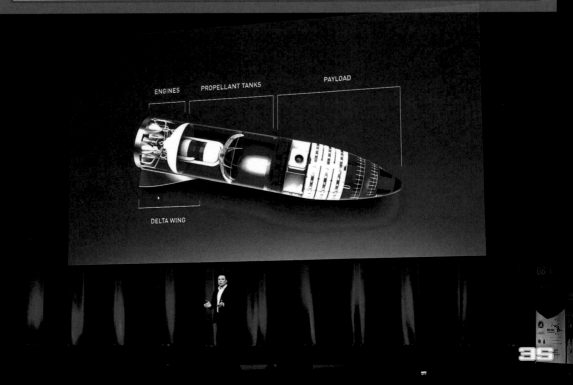

cities on Earth. Because all parts of the rocket and spaceship are reusable, costs will be greatly reduced.

As an entrepreneur, Musk thinks in terms of cost. He hopes to make a colonist's move to Mars cost about the same as the median US house price. He envisions people saving up just as they would for a home on Earth. And he's not picky about who colonizes. Musk declares, "Almost anyone, if they saved up and this was their goal, could buy a ticket and move to Mars." Musk makes no promises about the time frame, but says that, with the new rocket, SpaceX could launch the first cargo mission to Mars by 2022. Two years later, they could launch four BFRs to Mars—two carrying people and two carrying cargo.

Zubrin's Mars Direct plan shares some features with Musk's plan. Zubrin is impressed by Musk's methane with oxygen propellant, which is both inexpensive and easy to make on Mars, and his reusable flight systems. But he identifies some flaws. For example, Musk proposes returning the spacecraft's relatively spacious habitat back to Earth, meaning it would be reused only once every four years. Instead, Zubrin suggests, the habitat could remain on Mars as the colonists' living quarters. This option would save fuel on the return trip and construction costs on Mars. Similarly, the rocket's massive second stage need not travel all the way to Mars. It could be released from the habitat once they both escape Earth's gravity. The second stage would travel only as far as the moon and then return to Earth. In this way, it could be reused for five launches in four years, instead of only one.

Early space travel involved only government agencies such as NASA. But for Mars colonization, NASA would cooperate with both private companies and other space agencies. NASA engineers are currently testing the Space Launch System (SLS), the most powerful rocket ever built. NASA's 2015 report, "Journey to Mars," reveals a plan for a permanent, independent colony on Mars by 2030. Tests are already

ORION AND THE SLS

NASA's newest technology for space travel is the *Orion* spacecraft, which will take astronauts as far as Mars and the asteroids. It will be propelled into space by the Space Launch System (SLS). In 2014, the *Orion* capsule's critical safety systems were tested successfully. In 2017, astronauts tested *Orion* in the Gulf of Mexico to evaluate exit procedures in case of an emergency after splash-down. The SLS's first mission, EM-1, will launch in 2019 without a crew from Cape Canaveral, Florida. It will travel beyond the moon and splash down in the Pacific Ocean. The mission will test the ability of ground crews to work together with the *Orion* spacecraft and SLS.

being done on the ISS. Later tests will be done in orbit around the moon. These early missions will allow major problems to be worked out near Earth. Later missions will occur in Mars orbit or on the Martian moons. The final step will be landing on Mars. NASA is working on a transportation system that uses solar electric energy to push spacecraft farther into space. This system will provide efficient transportation to ferry supplies to Mars months or years before astronauts land. NASA is also developing more powerful rovers, such as RASSOR.

Another important part of space colonization research involves health issues caused by living for extended periods in space, including cancer due to radiation exposure and eyesight problems, as microgravity increases pressure in the optic nerve. Identical twin astronauts Scott and Mark Kelly are providing NASA with invaluable data on the effects of space travel on health. In 2015 and 2016, Scott spent 340 days

How will long-term life in space affect the human body? Results of a NASA study comparing identical twin astronauts, Scott (*left*) and Mark Kelly, will benefit future space colonists.

on the ISS, while Mark remained on Earth. The same factors were monitored in both twins, including sleep patterns, heart rate, immune response, fine motor skills, metabolism, and gut bacteria. Because the twins are genetically identical, the study also provides a unique opportunity to study how space affects DNA. Comparing their reactions will help doctors understand how space affects health and help them prepare astronauts for the nine-month journey to Mars.

Scientists understand the challenges required to get humans to Mars and develop colonies there. But they are determined, and the scientific and technological expertise is accumulating. No one can know the exact date, but perhaps by 2030, Elon Musk's vision will become reality, and humans will become a multiplanetary species.

CHAPTER 5

MOVING OUT: ASTEROIDS AND PLANETS

Detailed plans exist for moon and Mars missions, and research and testing are underway. But space scientists and engineers are also looking to colonize more distant regions. Plans already exist for colonizing asteroids. The moons of Jupiter and Saturn may not be far behind.

ASTEROIDS AND NEOS

A band of rocks, the asteroid belt, orbits between Mars and Jupiter. Ten billion asteroids are larger than 328 feet (100 m). Another one hundred billion are much smaller. An unknown number of near-Earth objects (NEOs)—including comets and asteroids—orbit close to Earth. Nearly all asteroids are filled with resources: carbon, nitrogen, ice, and metals including iron, nickel, and platinum. Their composition varies, but asteroids are rich in the resources needed for space colonies. In addition, asteroids could replenish resources on a depleted Earth. This possibility would require dependable transport. A transport system will likely involve permanently orbiting spacecraft running on a predictable schedule between asteroid mines and Earth.

Vesta, shown in a photo taken by NASA's *Dawn* spacecraft, is the second-largest known asteroid, at 330 miles (530 km) across. Several fragments of Vesta have reached Earth as meteorites.

Science fiction writer Isaac Asimov suggested hollowing out asteroids and setting up colonies inside them. The rocky surface would protect against radiation and micrometeorites. Interior areas perpendicular to the axis of rotation would have artificial gravity. An up-to-date version of this approach is the Dyson Asteroid Shell (DAS), which completely encloses the asteroid in a rigid or semirigid shell. A pressurized, breathable atmosphere is pumped in, and colonists live and work freely on or under the asteroid surface. The shell protects from radiation and stabilizes the asteroid during mining. Slowly, as the asteroid is mined out, a hollow permanent habitat is formed inside.

THE CYCLER: MAKING SPACE TRANSPORT ROUTINE

Astronaut and engineer Buzz Aldrin was the second man to walk on the moon. But Aldrin did not like the plant-a-flag-and-leave approach of the Apollo moon landings. He envisioned a future where solar system space travel was routine. Just as people do not drive a car to one location and abandon it, so spacecraft should be reused. Aldrin's solution was the cycler, a permanently orbiting spacecraft that cycles on a predictable schedule between two locations—Earth and Mars, for example, or Earth and the asteroid belt. The cycler accelerates only once, to achieve a solar orbit that passes both locations. Then, it coasts through space on its own momentum, gaining thrust each time it swings by a space body. A system of cyclers would allow routine transport of people and cargo between Earth and space destinations. This approach would greatly decrease the cost and energy required for space travel. Elon Musk's BFR system has similarities to Aldrin's cycler.

The gravity balloon combines aspects of a hollow asteroid and an artificial habitat. Large asteroids would not require a hardened pressure vessel such as the DAS to be habitable. An asteroid's center could be hollowed out, lined with plastic sheeting, and filled with air. The asteroid inflates, forming a gravity balloon. Many asteroids have less mass than predicted by their surface area, suggesting caves within them. Filling these caves with air would further increase workable space. Building a gravity balloon requires precise mathematics to balance the mining activities that clear space with the production of air.

Space colonies, either artificial or asteroid based, also need gravity. Planet-sized rotating space stations described in science fiction would be inefficient and power intensive. The fictional world in Karl Schroeder's book *Sun of Suns* has smaller rotating rings floating freely inside a giant, pressurized habitat. To attain Earth gravity, this three-dimensional space city would need to rotate at more than one hundred miles per hour (161 kmh), generating hurricane-force winds. A physicist (writing anonymously at SciFiIdeas.com) suggests a way to overcome this problem on a gravity-balloon habitat. He would surround a rotating cylinder with ten to twenty successive layers of plastic sheeting, dividing the air flow and lowering air resistance. To eliminate turbulence, the ends of the sheets would be tapered. This method would provide entry or exit points between gravity and zero-gravity regions. This combination of artificial gravity and central asteroid pressure would allow both breathing and Earth gravity without excess weight or great material strength.

COLONIZING DISTANT MOONS

Science fiction writers, including Arthur C. Clarke (*2010: Odyssey Two*), Gregory Benford (*Against Infinity*), and Donald Moffitt (*The Jupiter Theft*), wrote about human colonization of Jupiter's moons. Arthur C. Clarke (*Imperial Earth*), Piers Anthony (*Bio of a Space Tyrant*), Stephen Baxter (*Titan*), and Stanislaw Lem (*Fiasco*) envisioned human colonies on Saturn's moons. Science may be catching up with science fiction.

Recent probes to Jupiter and Saturn give tantalizing glimpses of rocky moons that might someday support human colonists. The *Galileo* spacecraft orbited Jupiter for seven years, 1996 to 2003. It provided detailed information on Jupiter's four largest moons. The *Cassini* spacecraft, launched in October 1997, entered Saturn orbit on July 1, 2004. On September 15, 2017, *Cassini* plunged into Saturn's atmosphere, ending its nearly twenty-year mission. It collected data on Saturn, its rings, and many of its sixty-two moons.

Three of Jupiter's four largest moons (Europa, Ganymede, and Callisto) are likely candidates for colonization, as are at least two of Saturn's (Enceladus and Titan). These moons all have water, in the form of very salty subsurface oceans. Europa's sea is covered

Just before ending its mission by crashing into Saturn, NASA's *Cassini* spacecraft took this final photo of Saturn's giant moon, Titan, which is covered by a dense atmosphere.

with water ice. Of Jupiter's moons, Callisto is NASA's first choice for colonization. Its dark surface and carbon dioxide (CO_2) atmosphere make it warmer than the others. The moons all appear to be rich in resources, and several (Callisto, Enceladus, and Titan) have abundant organic compounds. Titan has a thick atmosphere that shields its surface from radiation. Besides its subsurface saltwater ocean, Titan also has surface oceans of liquid methane.

The three greatest challenges to colonizing Jupiter's moons are radiation, low temperatures, and distance. Radiation around Jupiter and its moons is deadly but decreases with distance from the planet. Radiation shielding would likely be the greatest challenge facing colonists. Temperatures in deep space are extremely cold—near absolute zero. Advances in shielding technology would be required to provide protection from both low temperatures and radiation. Despite their greater distance, Saturn's moons seem better for colonization because Saturn has much less radiation. Titan falls outside Saturn's radiation belt and also has a thick atmosphere that could shield colonists from cosmic rays.

Finally, there is distance. Using twenty-first century spaceflight technologies, a trip from Earth to the moon takes two to three days. A trip to Mars takes six to nine months. Jupiter averages 391 million miles (630 million km) from Earth. A trip to colonize Jupiter would take more than six years. Saturn is even more distant. Because of its elliptical orbit, it ranges from 746 million miles (1.2 billion km) to 1.1 billion miles (1.7 billion km) from Earth. The *Voyager I* probe reached Saturn in thirty-eight months; however, a colony ship would take considerably longer. Scientists are looking at new technologies, such as in ion propulsion, which creates thrust by pushing ions with electricity. This highly efficient technology eliminates the need for chemical fuel. In NASA's High Power Electric Propulsion (HiPEP) project, tests reached velocities greater than two hundred thousand miles per hour (90,000 m/s). With this

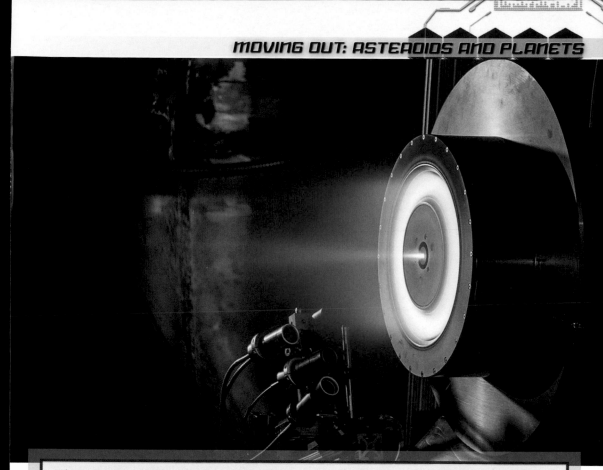

This prototype 13-kilowatt Hall thruster, being tested at NASA's Glenn Research Center, in Cleveland, is a key development in NASA's High Power Electric Propulsion project (HiPEP).

technology, plus lighter spacecraft, travel to Jupiter could take less than a year.

Discoveries by unpeopled probes have sparked intense interest in the moons of Jupiter and Saturn. For the next century or more, adventurers, scientists, and engineers will be focused on colonizing the solar system—the moon, Mars, the asteroid belt, and possibly even these distant moons. Musk's BFR system could be expanded to involve moving materials to and from the moons of Jupiter and Saturn. But, without a breakthrough in spacefaring technology (which could happen but cannot be predicted), humans will remain within the solar system for the foreseeable future.

CHAPTER 6

THE ETHICS OF COLONIZING PLANETS

At the founding convention of the Mars Society in 1998, Dr. Robert Zubrin said colonizing Mars was comparable to pioneering the American West—it would create jobs and opportunities and relieve population pressures. He even said humans have a duty, or a moral obligation, to terraform Mars into a new Earth, because "it is the Western tradition to expand continually and to value humans above nature."

People like Zubrin are called anthropocentric or "human centered." They believe everything on Earth exists for the benefit of humans and that humans should dominate life. Zubrin extends this viewpoint to domination of space. Biocentrism, by contrast, is "life centered." This environmental viewpoint says all life has value, regardless of its usefulness to humans. Now that humans are expanding outward to other worlds, some think the field of ethics should be broadened even further.

David Grinspoon, writing for *Slate*, the online magazine, warns strongly against applying anthropocentric attitudes to space exploration. "Is this really the way we want to frame our dreams of inhabiting Mars?" he asks. He points out that colonizing Mars (or any other world) would not only affect science. It would have

BEYOND BIOCENTRISM

Environmental ethicist Keekok Lee advocates going beyond biocentrism, to consider the intrinsic value of abiotic or inanimate nature. Her argument is constructed for Earth but can be extended to Mars. Lee points out that Earth did not come into existence for the benefit of humans. Although humans use much of nature, nature does not exist solely for them. Earth's formation occurred independently of their arrival, and its other forms of life would not disappear if humans went extinct. From the perspective of Earth and its life, she says, humans are nonessential, possibly even redundant.

historic and spiritual importance and should be approached with humanistic goals and environmental consciousness. But will people slow down their plans to colonize new worlds long enough to consider these broader implications?

WHO OWNS OTHER PLANETS?

Many advocates of colonization point to the warnings of Stephen Hawking, Elon Musk, and others. They assume a disaster will eventually destroy Earth and civilization. They see Mars as Earth's "backup planet." A permanent Mars settlement could preserve a few people, animals, and plants, plus records of human history. These advocates see colonizing Mars as the only morally responsible option. But who owns

Mars? Can the Mars Society claim it? Can the United States or some other country? The first country (or company) to land there? Who owns asteroids or the moons of Jupiter or Saturn? The issue of space ownership is serious, for both mining and colonization purposes.

The Outer Space Treaty of 1967 is an international treaty that describes space as "the provenance of all mankind." This notion means no country can rule any space body. According to Jacob Haqq-Misra, director of the Blue Marble Space Institute of Science in Seattle, this view makes it difficult for companies with space mining plans, who anticipate big profits. Between 2027 and 2032, the firm Planetary Resources plans to be mining asteroids for water, from which they will extract hydrogen and oxygen. They plan to market these resources to later missions at space "gas stations." According to Chris Lewicki, chief executive of Planetary Resources, "If you obtain a resource and bring it with you, it becomes your property."

Lewicki bases his assumption not on the Outer Space Treaty but on later laws passed by individual nations. In 2015, the United States passed legislation allowing private US companies to own space resources. In 2017, Luxembourg passed similar laws giving private firms own-

President Lyndon B. Johnson (*right*) was one of several world leaders signing the Outer Space Treaty of 1967, which banned space weapons and ownership of space bodies by any country.

ership of resources mined in space. But experts hope space resource rights will eventually be based on a legal framework similar to the United Nations Law of the Sea Convention. This convention says oceans are not owned by any country, but all countries have exclusive rights to harvest resources in a given region around their coastlines. In space, a country (or company) might receive exclusive rights for a given area around its landing point but not for the entire planet. Attorney Andrew Brehm says, "Outer space is viewed in society as something similar to the ocean, where there is a collective interest … A first come, first serve system does not necessarily work well when only certain countries or private entities can (currently) reach outer space."

ETHICS OF ASTEROID MINING

Space ownership would not affect only those people wealthy enough to run a space mining operation. Space mining could have major implications back on Earth. Robert Lamb, on the website Seeker,

Brother Guy Consolmagno, an astronomer at the Vatican Observatory, in Castel Gandolfo, near Rome, holds a Mars meteorite. He is an expert on connections between meteorites and asteroids.

describes the views of Jesuit brother Guy Consolmagno, who works as a research astronomer and planetary scientist at the Vatican Observatory. Brother Consolmagno asks what would happen to resource-exporting nations on Earth if asteroid mining began to bring in huge profits. How would the cost of iron and other ores change? Would Earth's mining and manufacturing industries be outsourced to space? If so, how many people would lose their jobs?

Tony Milligan, of England's University of Hertfordshire, notes that an asteroid mining boom would cause a sudden influx of resources to Earth, destabilizing economies. A system of regulations would feed resources from asteroids into the Earth system more slowly, destabilizing economies less. Such a system was proposed in John L. Lewis's 1996 book, *Mining the Sky*. Milligan suggests that, although asteroid mining might ease resource depletion on Earth, it would not help most people. It would probably make the rich even richer.

Milligan sees many ethical problems tied to asteroid mining. First, mining is dangerous on Earth and would be even more dangerous in space. Second, the dependency of workers in extreme hostile environments (such as space) often results in authoritarian governments. Milligan explains, "Whoever controls the air supply and infrastructure could control the people." Finally, mining is environmentally destructive. Do ethical, responsible people destroy a planet (or unique parts of it) simply because they can?

NEW PLANETS, TERRAFORMING, AND LIFE

As soon as humans set foot on another world, it begins to change. Neil Armstrong and Buzz Aldrin left footprints on the moon. Mars rovers make tracks through Martian soil. Colonists will mine resources and build habitats and roads. Most Mars planners envision terraforming Mars by generating a breathable atmosphere, producing liquid water, and significantly raising the temperature. This process would probably include melting the polar ice caps by generating a runaway greenhouse effect. Moreover, humans will bring Earth microorganisms with them. All organisms carry their own communities of microorganisms, or microbiomes, with them. Even if possible, sterilizing spacecraft and other items would not help.

Every human activity on another planet leaves traces. Here, on February 19, 2014, the Mars *Curiosity* rover looks back and photographs its own wheel tracks.

If a planet has no life (even bacteria), many people see no ethical problem with exploiting or terraforming it. But is this view too simplistic? Would people be justified in destroying the Grand Canyon or turning it into an inland sea? How about Valles Marineris, the Grand Canyon of Mars? Paul York, writing for *Philosophy Now*, notes that the failure of ethics to consider nonliving things (such as mountains, rivers, or canyons) has mattered little, because on Earth, these things are home to living organisms. But this will not be true for all planets. York advocates extending ethics to nonliving systems, to help limit the arrogance of anthropocentrism. He says nonliving planets have their own intrinsic value, greater than any economic value humans assign to them. This belief does not mean banning colonization. It does mean extending environmental responsibility to other planets.

As scientists learn more about both solar system neighbors and exoplanets, it seems more and more likely that life exists elsewhere. Water and organic molecules occur on many planets and moons, including Mars. If a planet does have life, even microscopic life, the stakes are even higher. Earth biology may be incompatible with alien life, resulting in the death of one or the other. Or a planet may have the ingredients necessary for life, but life has not yet formed. Should humans leave this planet alone, and allow it to evolve naturally? In the far future, people may have to deal with the implications of colonizing a planet with intelligent life. They may even adopt *Star Trek*'s Prime Directive, which prohibits interference with other cultures and civilizations. Until such time as life is discovered somewhere other than Earth, there is much work to do on simpler ethical problems.

TIMELINE

1912 Edgar Rice Burroughs serializes *A Princess of Mars* in a sci-fi magazine; in 1917, he will publish it as the first of eleven books in his Barsoom (Mars) series featuring John Carter.

1942 The first book of Isaac Asimov's Foundation series, chronicling a galaxy-wide civilization, is published; he will write six more books, with the last published in 1993.

1950 Ray Bradbury's book *The Martian Chronicles* is published.

1957 The Soviet Union launches *Sputnik 1* on October 4.

1966 The original *Star Trek* series debuts on television.

1967 The Outer Space Treaty is formed; it described space as "the provenance of all mankind."

1969 NASA's *Apollo 11* lands on the moon on July 20; US astronauts Neil Armstrong and Buzz Aldrin become the first humans to walk on the moon.

1972 *Pioneer 10* is launched toward Jupiter.

1977 The first *Star Wars* movie is released on May 25.

1981 The first space shuttle flight (*Columbia*) occurs; the program will last for thirty years, until 2011.

1996 The *Galileo* probe goes into orbit around Jupiter, where it will remain until 2003.

2000 Beginning on November 2, the ISS has a permanent crew of six onboard.

2004 The *Cassini* probe enters orbit around Saturn on July 1, where it will remain until September 15, 2017.

2009 The Kepler Space Telescope, the planet-hunting telescope, is launched in March.

2022 A group of partners including NASA, ESA, SpaceX, and Bigelow Aerospace could put ten settlers on the moon by this date, according to a 2015 study.

2030 NASA says a Mars mission with a crew could occur by this date.

GLOSSARY

anthropocentrism The human-centered view that everything on Earth (and by extension, in space) exists for the benefit of humans and that humans should dominate life and nonlife.

asteroid A small, rocky body orbiting the sun; most asteroids orbit in the asteroid belt, a ring between the orbits of Mars and Jupiter.

biocentrism The life-centered view that all life has intrinsic importance, regardless of its usefulness to humans.

cryogenic Relating to very low temperatures.

cycler A permanently orbiting spacecraft that cycles on a regular schedule between two locations, such as Earth and Mars; it accelerates only once, to reach solar orbit, and then moves by momentum, making it highly energy efficient.

Dyson Asteroid Shell A rigid or semirigid shell enclosing an asteroid to provide a pressurized, breathable atmosphere for asteroid mining; currently a concept, not a reality.

entrepreneur A person who designs, organizes, and runs one or more businesses and assumes the financial risk for their success.

exoplanet A planet revolving around another sun, that is, a planet outside the solar system, at a distance of light-years from Earth.

gravity balloon A concept proposed to enclose an asteroid's interior space in plastic sheets filled with air, to provide air pressure and a breathable atmosphere for both mining and habitats.

hard science fiction Science fiction in which the science is required and integral to the story; often based on extensions of current science or hypotheses of new science.

low earth orbit (LEO) An orbit extending from Earth's surface up to 1,200 miles (1,931 km); used for most communication satellites because the energy required to get them into orbit is less than for higher orbits.

magnetic field A region around a magnetic material or an electrical charge where the force of magnetism acts; a magnetic field has both direction and magnitude (strength).

magnetosphere A region of space surrounding an astronomical object (sun, planet, and so forth) where charged particles are controlled by the object's magnetic field.

Mars rover A robotic vehicle, fitted with cameras and scientific equipment, that moves independently over the Martian surface collecting scientific data and transmitting it to Earth.

microbiome The set of populations of microorganisms living in a specific environment, such as the human body.

near-Earth object (NEO) An asteroid or comet orbiting in Earth's neighborhood; a few orbit close enough to be considered potential hazards.

regolith The layer of loose material covering bedrock on Earth or another planet; it may contain some combination of soil, dust, sand, loose gravel, rock fragments, and volcanic ash.

soft science fiction Science fiction in which science is present but not central; it concentrates more on the effect of science on the sociology or behavior of people and societies.

solar energetic particles (SEPs) Highly energetic particles of radiation released by the sun during solar flares.

terraforming Planetary engineering; physically transforming a planet to make it more like Earth or more able to support life, for example, increasing atmospheric density or adding oxygen to the atmosphere.

zero gravity (zero-G) The situation in which no gravity is acting on an object or organism, and it floats freely; for example, zero-G operates in space, where no space body (such as Earth) is close enough to exert gravity.

Canadian Space Agency
John H. Chapman Space Centre
6767 Route de l'Aéroport
Saint-Hubert, QC J3Y 8Y9
Canada
(450) 926-4800
Website: http://www.asc-csa.gc.ca
/eng/default.asp
Facebook: @CanadianSpaceAgency
Instagram: @canadianspaceagency
Twitter: @csa_asc
The Canadian Space Agency is
committed to the peaceful use
and development of space,
the increase of knowledge
about space through scientific
research, and the use of space
science and technology for the
benefit of Canadians.

Canadian Space Society
14356 Churchill Road North
Acton, ON L7J2L8
Canada
Website: https://css.ca
Facebook: @CanadianSpaceSociety
Instagram: @canadianspacesociety
Twitter: @CdnSpaceSociety
The Canadian Space Society is a
nonprofit organization of pro-
fessionals, students, and space
enthusiasts dedicated to the
human exploration of space,

including the solar system
and beyond.

European Space Agency (ESA)
Communication Department
8-10 rue Mario Nikis
75738 Paris
Cedex 15
France
+33 1 5369 7155
Website: http://www.esa.int/ESA
Facebook: @EuropeanSpaceAgency
Instagram: @europeanspaceagency
Twitter: @esa
The ESA is an intergovernmental
agency involving twenty-two
European countries and head-
quartered in Paris, France. It
launches exploration missions
to the moon and planets, car-
ries out observations of Earth,
and is active in science and
telecommunications.

Federation of Galaxy Explorers
(FOGE)
6404 Ivy Lane, Suite 810
Greenbelt, MD 20770
(610) 981-8511
Website: http://www.foge.org
Facebook: @FederationOfGalaxy-
Explorers
Twitter: @GalaxyExplorers

FOGE is a US youth group that seeks to inspire and educate young people for a future that involves space exploration. It teaches space-related science and engineering. Projects include after-school Mission Team meetings on science and technology that award medals and certificates for participation and Moon Base and Mars Base summer camps.

Mars Society
11111 West 8th Avenue, Unit A
Lakewood, CO 80215
(303) 980-0890
Website: http://www.marssociety.org
Facebook, Instagram, and Twitter: @TheMarsSociety
The Mars Society was founded to further the exploration and settlement of Mars. It seeks to educate the public, media, and government on the benefits of exploring and colonizing Mars.

National Aeronautics and Space Administration (NASA)
NASA Headquarters
300 E. Street SW, Suite 5R30
Washington, DC 20546
(202) 358-0001
Website: https://www.nasa.gov
Facebook: @NASA
Instagram, and Twitter: @nasa
NASA is the US space agency. It is responsible for the civilian space program and for research into aeronautics and aerospace. The website includes a gallery of space images, general information on space, and information on each of NASA's many space missions, including the ISS and Mars missions.

Space Frontier Foundation
4539 Seminary Road
Alexandria, VA 22304
Website: https://spacefrontier.org
Facebook: @SpaceFrontier
Twitter: @SpaceFrontier and @newspacenews
This foundation is dedicated to expanding the human species into space through colonization as rapidly as possible. It wants to "unleash the power of free enterprise" while also "protecting the Earth's fragile biosphere and creating a freer and more prosperous life" for succeeding generations through the use of space resources.

FOR FURTHER READING

Aldrin, Buzz, with Marianne J. Dyson. *Welcome to Mars: Making a Home on the Red Planet*. Washington, DC: National Geographic, 2015.

Dinks, Brain. *Space Exploration and Colonization*. Seattle, WA: Amazon Digital Services LLC, 2015.

Green, Carl R. *Walking on the Moon. The Amazing Apollo 11 Mission*. Berkeley Heights, NJ: Enslow Publishing, 2013.

Hand, Carol. *Is There Life Out There? The Likelihood of Alien Life and What It Would Look Like*. New York, NY: Rosen Publishing, 2016.

Harmon, Daniel E. *The Early Days of Space Exploration*. New York, NY: Britannica Educational Publishing, 2018.

Hernández Pamplona, Alberto. *A Visual Guide to Space Exploration*. New York, NY: Rosen Publishing, 2018.

Holden, Henry M. *The Coolest Job in the Universe. Working Aboard the International Space Station*. Berkeley Heights, NJ: Enslow Publishing, 2013.

Ingram, Dennis. *Foothold: The Story of Mankind's First Expedition to the Stars*. Amazon Digital Services LLC, 2014.

Kilby, Gerald M. *Colony One Mars (Colony Mars Book 1)*. 3rd ed. Seattle, WA: Amazon Digital Services LLC, 2017.

Paul, T S. *The Martian Inheritance* (Athena Lee Chronicles Book 7). Seattle, WA: Amazon Digital Services LLC, 2016.

Petrikowski, Nicki Peter. *Critical Perspectives on the Viability of Human Life on Other Planets*. New York, NY: Enslow Publishing, 2017.

Porterfield, Jason. *The Benefits of Spaceflight and Space Exploration*. New York, NY: Rosen Publishing, 2018.

Ruth, Michael. *Space Exploration*. Farmington Hills, MI: Greenhaven Press, 2016.

Wright, Bill, and Doug Turnbull. *We Are the Martians: A Guide for the Colonization of the Planet Mars*. Inter-Planet Books, Sold by Amazon Digital Services LLC, 2016.

BIBLIOGRAPHY

Alan (Guest). "Gravity Balloons: Colonizing the Asteroid Belt." SciFi Ideas. com, December 5, 2013. http://www.scifiideas.com/science-2 /colonizing-asteroid-cores.

Bennett, Jay. "First Private Moon Landing Gears Up for Launch by Year's End." *Popular Mechanics*, June 2, 2017. http://www .popularmechanics.com /space/moon-mars/a26702/moon-express -lunar-landing-launch-years-end.

Charania, A. C. "Dyson Asteroid Shells: Hollow Worlds from the Out-side-In." SpaceWorks Engineering, Inc. Retrieved September 8, 2017. http://www.sei.aero/eng/papers/uploads/archive/ISTS_2008 _DysonAsteroidShell_paper_v4.pdf.

Dinkin, Sam. "Colonize the Moon before Mars." *Space Review*, September 7, 2004. http://www.thespacereview.com/article/221/1.

Fecht, Sarah. "Colonizing the Moon May Be 90 Percent Cheaper Than We Thought." *Popular Science*, July 20, 2015. http://www.popsci.com/col-onizing-moon-may-be-90-percent-cheaper-we-thought.

Frazier, Sarah. "Real Martians: How to Protect Astronauts from Space Radiation on Mars." NASA, September 30, 2015 (updated August 4, 2017). https://www.nasa.gov/feature/goddard/real-martians-how-to -protect-astronauts-from-space-radiation-on-mars.

Ginsberg, Leah. "Elon Musk Thinks Life on Earth Will Go Extinct, and Is Putting Most of His Fortune Toward Colonizing Mars." CNBC, June 16, 2017. http://www.cnbc.com/2017/06/16/elon-musk -colonize-mars-before-extinction-event-on-earth.html.

Gramuglia, Anthony. "History of Science Fiction Part III." Futurism .media. Retrieved September 8, 2017. https://futurism.media/history -of-science-fiction-part-iii.

Grinspoon, David H. "Is Mars Ours? The Logistics and Ethics of Coloniz-ing the Red Planet." *Slate*, January 7, 2004. http://www.slate.com /articles/health_and_science/science/2004/01/is_mars_ours.html.

Kerwick, Thomas B. "Colonizing Jupiter's Moons: An Assessment of Our Options and Alternatives." Washington Academy of Sciences.

Retrieved September 8, 2017. http://www.environmental-safety.webs
.com/Galileo_WaS_Journal.pdf.

Kluger, Jeffrey. "What *The Martian* Gets Right (and Wrong) About
Science." *Time*, May 18, 2016. http://time.com/4055413
/martian-movie-review-science-accuracy-matt-damon.

Knapton, Sarah. "Nasa Planning 'Earth Independent' Mars Colony by
2030s." *The Telegraph*, October 9, 2015. http://www.telegraph.co.uk
/science/2016/03/14/nasa-planning-earth-independent-mars
-colony-by-2030s.

Krauss, Lawrence M. *The Physics of Star Trek*. New York, NY: Basic Books,
A Division of HarperCollins Publishers, 1995.

Krugman, Paul. "Paul Krugman: Asimov's Foundation Novels Grounded
My Economics." *The Guardian*, December 4, 2012. https://www
.theguardian.com/books/2012/dec/04/paul-krugman-asimov
-economics.

Lamb, Robert. "The Ethics of Planetary Exploration and Colonization.
Seeker, February 17, 2010. https://www.seeker.com/the-ethics-of
-planetary-exploration-and-colonization-1765024740.html.

Liptak, Andrew. "How Science Fiction Has Imagined Colonizing Our Solar System and Beyond." *The Verge*, September 24, 2016. https://www
.theverge.com/2016/9/24/12999798/science-fiction-mars-spacex
-outer-space-colonization-theories.

MacDonald, Fiona. "NASA Scientists Say We Could Colonise the Moon
by 2022 for Just $10 Billion." *Science Alert*, March 22, 2016. http://
www.sciencealert.com/nasa-scientists-say-we-could-colonise-the
-moon-by-2022-for-just-10-billion.

McKie, Robin. "Life on Earth Is in Peril. We Have No Future If We Don't
Go into Space." *The Guardian*. December 7, 2014.
https://www.theguardian.com/science/2014/dec/07/space-probes-or
-manned-missions.

Milligan, Tony. "Asteroid Mining, Integrity and Containment."
Commercial Space Exploration: Ethics, Policy and Governance, edited by
Jai Galliott. Burlington, VT: Ashgate Publishing, 2015.

http://www.academia.edu/7564584/Asteroid_Mining_Integrity_and_Containment.

Research Summary. "Why Should We Colonize Other Planets?" The Benefits of Things. Retrieved September 8, 2017. https://www.benefitsof.org/why-should-we-colonize-other-planets.

Roberts, Andy. "10 Planets from The Star Wars Universe That Exist in Our Own." Listverse.com, April 18, 2015. http://listverse.com/2015/04/18/10-planets-from-the-star-wars-universe-that-exist-in-our-own.

Union of Concerned Scientists. "UCS Satellite Database." April 11, 2017. http://www.ucsusa.org/nuclear-weapons/space-weapons/satellite-database#.WY3dfem2w2w.

Walker, Robert. "Asteroid Resources Could Create Space Habs for Trillions; Land Area of a Thousand Earths." Science20.com, July 17, 2013. http://www.science20.com/robert_inventor/blog/asteroid_resources_could_create_space_habs_for_trillions_land_area_of_a_thousand_earths-116541.

Wall, Mike. "SpaceX's Mars Colony Plan: How Elon Musk Plans to Build a Million-Person Martian City." Space.com, June 14, 2017. https://www.space.com/37200-read-elon-musk-spacex-mars-colony-plan.html.

York, Paul. "The Ethics of Terraforming." *Philosophy Now*, Issue 121, August/September 2017. https://philosophynow.org/issues/38/The_Ethics_of_Terraforming.

Zubrin, Robert. "Colonizing Mars." *The New Atlantis*, October 21, 2016. http://www.thenewatlantis.com/publications/colonizing-mars.

Zubrin, Robert. "How Scientifically Accurate Is *The Martian*?" *The Guardian*, October 6, 2015. https://www.theguardian.com/film/2015/oct/06/how-scientifically-accurate-is-the-martian.

Zubrin, Robert. "The Promise of Mars." National Space Society, May/June 1996 (updated April 24, 2011). http://www.nss.org/settlement/mars/zubrin-promise.html.

INDEX

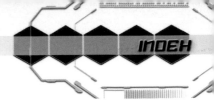

ABOUT THE AUTHOR

Carol Hand has a PhD in zoology with a specialization in marine ecology. She has taught college biology, worked for standardized testing companies, developed multimedia science and technology curricula (including titles on life science and astronomy), and written numerous science and technology books for young people. She follows space exploration closely and keenly anticipates both space colonization and the discovery of alien life.

PHOTO CREDITS

Cover, p. 1, pp. 4, 7, 16, 23, 32, 39, 46 (planets and stars) NikoNomad/Shutterstock.com; p. 5 NASA/JPL-Caltech/Cornell University/Arizona State University; p. 8 Time Life Pictures /The LIFE Picture Collection/Getty Images; pp. 10, 12 Photo 12 /Alamy Stock Photo; p. 11 CBS Photo Archive/Getty Images; pp. 17, 51 NASA/JPL-Caltech; pp. 19, 20, 27, 30, 33, 45 NASA; p. 25 Encyclopaedia Britannica/Universal Images Group/Getty Images; p. 28 NASA/David C. Bowman; p. 35 Mark Brake/Getty Images; p. 38 © AP Images; p. 40 NASA/JPL-Caltech/UCLA /MPS/DLR/IDA; p. 43 NASA/JPL-Caltech/Space Science Institute; p. 48 Corbis Historical/Getty Images; p. 49 Vincenzo Pinto /AFP/Getty Images; back cover and interior pages (circular element), interior pages (circuit board) Titima Ongkantong/ Shutterstock.com

Design: Nelson Sá; Layout: Tahara Anderson; Senior Editor: Kathy Kuhtz Campbell; Photo Research: Nicole DiMella